CAR SPRAYING MADE EASY

CAR SPRAYING
MADE EASY

CECIL JASPER
Author of 'How to Paint Boats'

LONDON
W. FOULSHAM & CO. LTD.
LONDON · TORONTO · CAPETOWN · SYDNEY

W. FOULSHAM & CO. LTD.
Yeovil Road, Slough, Bucks., England

ISBN 0 572 00031 6

© *Copyright* W. FOULSHAM AND CO. LTD. 1965
Printed and bound in Great Britain by
REDWOOD BURN LIMITED, TROWBRIDGE AND ESHER

CONTENTS

INTRODUCTION

Thousands of second-hand cars are sold each month.

The paintwork of many of these cars is drab and yet the bodywork and mechanical parts may be in a good condition. Shabby paintwork lowers the market value of any car.

Paint is always a good investment and a protection against rust. The cost of professional spraying is high and not all professional work is good. Spray gun manufacturers, realizing this, have perfected spray equipment suitably and reasonably priced for the amateur sprayer.

More and more motorists would like to spray or paint their own cars. They have discovered that the job can be done at less than half the price charged by the trade.

This book is written to help the amateur car sprayer to give his car a smart, plate-glass finish easily and economically.

CECIL JASPER

CHAPTER 1

THE TOOLS YOU NEED

Many car owners now realize the value of paint spraying equipment. Not all of them know that it is possible to spray one's own car at less than half the cost charged by garages.

Patience and practice bring experience, but if the advice given in this book is conscientiously followed it is possible to do a satisfactory job even at the first attempt.

Many owners of second-hand cars do not have a lot of money to spend on spraying equipment. With a little ingenuity, however, and careful planning, it is quite surprising how an efficient spray plant can be fixed up. It is not always the most expensive equipment that produces the best work; in fact many professional sprayers use improvised equipment with good results.

Large stocks of materials are unnecessary. You can purchase your materials in small quantities. There is no need to lay out a lot of money.

It is most important to bear in mind that paints are divided into two main classes: the cellulose finish which dries rapidly, and the synthetic finish which dries more slowly.

Cellulose must never be applied over synthetic or any other type of finish, otherwise it will lift it. If in doubt always give the existing finish to be sprayed a coat of sealer beforehand. Remember this or you may have the job of stripping the existing paintwork. Cellulose and its thinners act as a solvent when sprayed over other paints.

It should also be clearly understood that no undercoat, resurfacer or finishing paint will adhere properly to a highly polished surface. The surface should be rubbed down to make it dull and give it a 'key' before paint is sprayed onto it. An old surface is often dirty and

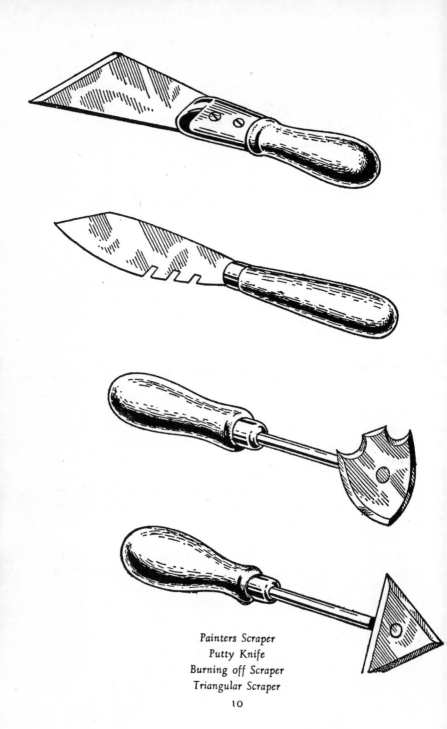

Painters Scraper
Putty Knife
Burning off Scraper
Triangular Scraper

10

greasy; it should be thoroughly cleaned down before painting other-wise the paint will not adhere to it.

A surface from which paint has been stripped must be rubbed down and cleaned before it has its first coat of primer. This has special properties for gripping the surface.

With a wood surface the matter is a little different, for the surface is not so smooth. But the object of forming a key for the paint should not be forgotten, so cleaning and rubbing down are important after all paint has been removed.

Tools Required

You will require: a painter's broad knife for stripping; a triangular scraper, handy for moving paint from corners and crevices when stripping; a flexible putty knife, useful for filling dents when stopping up.

A blowlamp for burning off old paintwork from wooden surfaces. A good car sponge, useful for wetting surface when wet rubbing down.

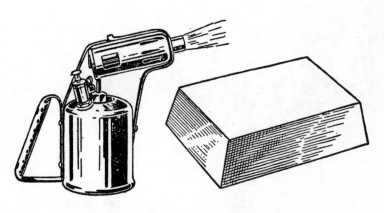

Blow Lamp   Wet Rubbing Down Stone

Washleather for wiping down paintwork and drying off the surface. One small bucket for clean water, clean rags for wiping dry, cotton wool for making rubber when polishing.

Steel graining combs, for combing over wet stain to produce simple grains. Ridgely graining tools, for mechanical graining.

Paint strainer, for straining dirty paint; an old nylon stocking is useful for this job.

Brushes for Brush Painting

A dusting brush, most essential for removing dust from all surfaces. One or two sable pencils, very useful for touching up and for painting letters on number plates.

One-inch, two-inch and three-inch flat varnish paint brushes, made by a reputable firm.

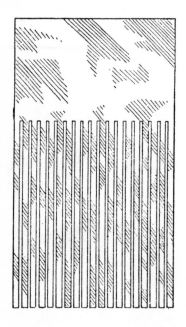
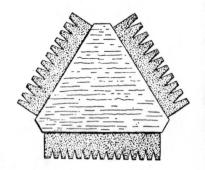

Steel Graining Comb
Rubber Graining Comb

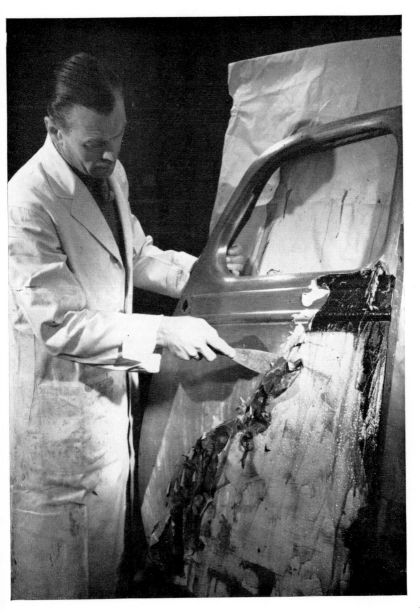

Stripping

Rubbing down wet

The Tools You Need

A wire brush for removing rust. A brush keeper for storing brushes when not in use; this can be made from an old colour tin. One stencil brush, for stencil letters and numbers.

Spraying Equipment

There are two main types of spraying equipment in use today: the first type employs a compressor, a container for the air, and a pressure-operated gun; this type is employed in factories for large-scale car spraying.

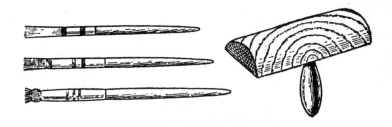

Overgraining Brushes · Graining Roller

Paint Strainer

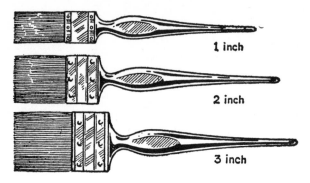

1 inch

2 inch

3 inch

Paint Brushes

Brush Keeper

The other type, used extensively by amateur car sprayers, makes use of volume instead of pressure. The air stream is produced by a blower unit or a vacuum cleaner.

One of the most popular spray guns in use today is the Burgess Electric Sprayer model V.S. 800, which costs 92/-. The complete equipment includes an electric sprayer with 24-ounce graduated container, and a four-ounce auxiliary touch-up container for small jobs.

There is also an angle nozzle adapter for directing the spray up and down, which saves tilting the sprayer. A paint strainer attachment automatically strains out dirt, grit and skin. The outfit includes a 15-ft. extension cord with spare parts kit, and an effective hand sander. The entire outfit in its carrying case weighs 8½ lbs.

The gun sprays all types of paint from cellulose to synthetic suitable for cars, and if kept clean is trouble-free. It has an adjustable knob for light or heavy spray, and a trigger 'off' switch. The operating mechanism is sealed in the shock-proof head of the gun.

A jar container holds the paint, and a pump forces this through the outlet tube past the spinner head, and out through the nozzle. The atomisation that results produces the fine pattern of droplets required for good car spraying.

The sprayer operates by pumping the paint out of the jar container rather than by building pressure in the container. This makes the outfit exceptionally safe to use, and the paint in the container is always visible.

Other Blower Spraying Units

Two other blower spraying units worth mentioning are made by Bylock Electric Ltd. No. 1. The Bylock Vortex Mark II, low-pressure unit, costs £9.7.6, and the Cyclone Spray Unit with Mark IV gun costs £13.13.0. Both are plug-in and spray units, and the weight of each unit is 14½ lbs.

These spraying outfits are precision built with three sizes of jets, adjustable nozzle atomiser, screw-top paint container, spare filter pad and set of prickers, made to suit all spraying requirements. Both these units are suitable for light industrial car spraying and should give good service if the filters are kept clean.

Other types of blower spray units are on the market with interchangeable nozzles, and considerable lengths of flexible cable. They can be used at good distances from the mains, and all these types have glass jar paint containers. At the base of each unit is a filter, which should be changed at intervals to prevent clogging up.

Provided it is powerful enough an ordinary vacuum cleaner can be used in place of a blower unit. The spray gun can be fixed to the blowing end of the vacuum cleaner by a 6 or 8ft. length of hose. The price of this is from 14/- to 21/-. Make sure the vacuum cleaner is free from dust.

Pressure Spraying Equipment

For the ambitious who wish to undertake a wider field of car spraying, pressure-spraying equipment used for industrial refinishing should prove satisfactory.

There is the high-pressure system and the low pressure; the latter is much better for the amateur. It means less wastage of spray material which reaches the surface with its full volatile content. This ensures good coverage and a good paint coating.

In pressure spraying the work is carried out by means of air taken from a container, air is pumped into this by a compressor driven by an electric or small petrol engine. It can be moved from place to place.

Pressure spraying equipment can be hired out from 15/- to £1.0.0 a day. This type of spray gun has interchangeable spray-heads, which can be changed immediately from a fine spray to a large shaped pattern.

The price of these spray guns varies from £18 to £56 or more according to the design. Instructions for operating are supplied by the makers.

Makers of Spray Equipment

Burgess Products Co. Ltd., Electric Tools Division, Sapcote, Leicester.

Bylock Electric Ltd., Enfield, Middlesex. Bylock and Vortex Spray Guns.

Bullows Ltd., Birmingham. Pressure Spray Guns.

Domestic Supply Co., 341 Regents Park, London.

Apparatus & Instrument Co., Ltd., 15 Sheen Lane, London, S.E.26.

CHAPTER 2

PAINTS AND MATERIALS

Buy your materials from a reputable firm, and use the brands selected throughout the entire job. Each paint maker designs his materials to go with one another. Materials by two different makers should not be mixed together. Remember this and costly mistakes will be avoided.

The two main classes of paints used for car spraying are cellulose and synthetic. Cellulose dries rapidly; synthetic, which can be applied by brush as well as spray, dries slowly. Cellulose and its thinners act as a solvent when placed over other paints; it will lift them. On the other hand synthetic can be sprayed over cellulose when dry. Cellulose can be polished to give a plate-glass finish, but this must be done gradually. Synthetic paint dries with a natural gloss, but can be polished when it loses its gloss.

These paints can be easily identified in shops, and instructions for use are on the labels of the tins. It is easy to identify cellulose paint—when you open the tin it smells like pear drops—but synthetic smells more like ordinary oil paint, or like turpentine. Paints for car spraying can be purchased from Halford's Stores, or from Lewis Berger stockists in all the large towns.

Cellulose Primer

This is the first coat of cellulose paint sprayed on bare metal from which the old paint has been stripped. The primer provides the key for the next coat, the resurfacer. The primer should be sprayed on in a thin coat. The colour is mostly grey or dull red. Zinc Chromate Primer is used for priming aluminium surfaces. This should be brushed on and allowed 24 hours in which to dry.

Resurfacer Coat, or Undercoat

The resurfacer coat—that is often called filler or undercoat—is sprayed over the priming coat. Its object is to obliterate and fill up and to provide a key for the finishing paint. It is made in various colours, grey being the most popular. It needs rubbing down when dry to obtain a smooth surface.

Thinners are employed for thinning cellulose materials; they have a pear-drop smell. Turpentine or turpentine substitute (white spirit) is used for thinning synthetic paints.

Car Stopper

This is sometimes called knife stopper. It is a thick, putty-like paste used for filling dents or abrasions. It should be used after the priming paint is dry. A painter's broad knife or scraper, or flexible putty knife, is the best tool for the application of stopping.

Car stopper should not be confused with filler, which means a thick undercoat or resurfacer placed over the priming coat.

Finishing Materials

Finishing materials, both cellulose and synthetic, are supplied in many colours, and there is also a clear cellulose, which acts as a kind of varnish when sprayed over cellulose, giving a quicker and better gloss when polished.

Smoothing Compound, or Cutting Paste

This is supplied in two grades, coarse and fine. It is designed to remove 'orange peel' or surface imperfections and so bring up the lustre of the finish. It should be used with a clean cloth pad, and the finished surface should be rubbed over evenly two or three days after final spraying. This can be followed with a good liquid car polish to produce a high glossy, smooth clean surface to which dirt or dust do not easily adhere.

Wax polish or other makes of polish are sold in 1-gallon, ½-gallon and 14-ounce tins. Wax polish should be applied evenly with a clean damp cloth. Allow to dry, then polish with a clean soft dry cloth free from lint. You must not wax for at least 2 or 3 weeks after painting or spraying it.

Degreaser or Cleaning Agent

This is used to remove oil, grease, tar or dirt from the surface before spraying. It should be rubbed over the surface, and finally washed off with clean water.

Paint Stripper or Paint Remover

This is used to remove old paint before spraying, which is essential when the surface is in a bad condition. The best type of paint stripper is non-toxic and non-inflammable. Although it is fairly safe to handle, eyes should be protected against splashes.

It should strip any known type of car finish, both cellulose and synthetic. One or two coats applied with an old paint brush will soften up the old paintwork in 10 to 15 minutes. The old paint is then removed with the stripping knife; it can be scraped or pushed off the surface in strips. The surface must be washed down with clean water immediately the paint is stripped, and all traces of stripper should be removed from corners, mouldings, and beadings. Afterwards rub down with 280 wet abrasive paper, then dry off with compressed air or clean rags.

Double strength Meltic Paint Remover is sold by all good paint stockists. Never remove old paint from a metal car body with a blow lamp, for the heat makes the surface contract or expand. A blow lamp, however, is very useful for burning paint from woodwork; the heat from the lamp fills up the grain of the wood and prevents moisture entering. Care should be taken not to scorch the woodwork. The flame of the lamp should be played on the surface carefully till the old paint softens up, then it can easily be scraped off.

Masking Tape, Masking Paste, and Fluid

Certain parts of a car need protecting while other parts are being sprayed. Masking tape is used for sticking on paper for this purpose. Difficult parts of the car can be given a coat of masking paste, or fluid, which can be washed off with any paint which has adhered to it. Brown paper is the best material for masking. A coat of whitening brushed on glass work also gives good protection and can be wiped off when the job is finished.

Rust Remover

This is a solution of mixed acids with good etching properties. Rubber gloves should be worn during application. It will remove all rust to ensure good adhesion of the paint, and chemically treat the surface of the metal to prevent further rusting. It should be applied to the rusted parts with a sponge and be left fifteen to twenty minutes. Afterwards rub over with abrasive paper to remove scale. Finally wash with water, wipe dry and spray on priming paint.

MATERIALS FOR WOOD

Red Lead Priming

This is a mixture of red lead and white lead, a traditional priming for all bare woodwork. It needs well stirring, and should be applied in a thin coat.

Shellac

This is used to seal up protruding knots before priming coat is applied. One or two coats will usually be sufficient. It dries quickly.

Undercoat

This is much the same as that used for spraying metal, the object being to fill up the grain of the wood and make a good foundation.

Finishing Paints

These are gloss paints and are weather-resisting. They should be applied on a warm day or in a temperature of 75 degrees. They work stiff under the brush and need plenty of distribution to prevent runs. Woodwork is much better if brush-painted; the paint can be well rubbed into the surface to fill up the grain.

Paints and Materials

Oil Graining Colour

This is known as scumble or graining colour and is made for staining over a buff painted ground, to give an oak effect. It is diluted with turpentine and should be applied with a stiff brush.

Black Japan

This makes a useful stain for bare wood when diluted with turps substitute. It is applied in the same way as scumble.

Filling Compound

This mixture can be rubbed into the surface with clean rags, before the woodwork is stained; afterwards the surplus is wiped off.

Oil stain, spirit stain and water stain are all sold with the other materials in paint shops. These materials are mostly used for staining new woodwork.

Wood lacquer is generally sprayed over stained and filled woodwork. Afterwards wood surface or clear cellulose is sprayed on to give a gloss.

Abrasives and Rubbing Down

Be sure that you do not use the wrong abrasives for rubbing down car bodies. This wastes time and labour. The grade of abrasive used is often too fine; it has a tendency to polish rather than cut and smooth.

The best abrasive should be coarse, provided it does not scratch and so expose priming or undercoat. 280 grade is suitable for rubbing down undercoating or resurfacer, and wet abrasive paper is best for the job.

'Abrasives', often called sandpaper, are made with different sizes and types of grit, and a different quality of backing. The number of the paper refers to the size of sieve through which the grit has passed. 500 is a very fine grit size, 280 is medium, and 120 is coarse.

'Wet and Dry' paper means that the sandpaper backing and glue are of the waterproof type, and can be used dry or with water. Abrasives for rubbing down car bodies are made with carborundum grit, which cuts paint much better than glass.

Glasspaper is very effective for cutting wood.

Garnet paper is an artificial grit with special rubbing-down properties for wood.

Emery paper, made with carborundum grit, is suitable for rubbing down metal.

Rubbing Down or Sanding

There is a correct way to rub down a car body, and the operation is not as easy as it appears to be. The rubbing down of the undercoat or resurfacer should always be done wet, and the best lubricant for this is soapy water, which tends to pick up material and become clogged.

Begin by thoroughly wetting the surface, then begin rubbing down with coarse paper. This produces a series of minute scratches and removes foreign matter. Follow on with fine abrasive paper. This removes the scratches made by the first abrasive and finally produces a series of extremely fine scratches. These are intermingled over the entire surface to give a key for the finishing coat.

The same process takes place on a wooden surface. The grain of the wood together with the pores forms a key. This sometimes raises the grain of the wood, which can be finally rubbed back smooth.

A smooth surface is the object of rubbing down. It is most important for a car body.

Technique of Rubbing

The rubbing can be done in a straight or circular motion, covering small areas at a time to blend the whole together. To ensure even pressure the fingers of the hand holding the abrasive should be kept close together and flat on the surface.

The pressure on the paper will vary. In the first place with the coarse paper the pressure should be fairly heavy, but this should be reduced when the fine grade of paper is employed. The final rubbing done with the fine paper should be light and even.

Care should be taken when rubbing down undercoat or resurfacer, for it is very easy to miss a section, and this can affect the finish. Both cellulose and synthetic surfaces can be rubbed down to a very fine finish if care is used. Remember, the final job will depend largely on how well you rub down. The surface must be smoothed out to perfection. Use plenty of soapy water and patience if you wish to get that plate-glass finish.

Abrasive paper bites harder where there are sharp edges. Too much material can be rubbed off car bodies that have raised beading around or below the window level. Avoid this by rubbing beadings, mouldings, or edges first and flat surfaces last.

The final rubbing down of cellulose after using fine abrasive paper can be carried out with cutting compound. This is made into a paste for easy application, making it possible to obtain a fine surface. Cutting compound if left for a time is inclined to dry up. A mixture of paraffin and linseed oil added to it will restore its quality.

Synthetic Finish

For rubbing down a synthetic finish start with a coarse paper, and finish with a medium paper. The object is to leave a coarser 'key'. Unlike cellulose, synthetic paint has filling properties. For instance, scratches on synthetic surfaces will dry out and disappear, but not on cellulose.

Small imperfections on a synthetic surface are covered up because there is more flow in the material. To achieve this the surface must have ample resurfacer coats, and be well rubbed down.

Wooden Surfaces

A wood surface is best rubbed down dry. This helps to fill up the grain of the wood. The surface must be thoroughly wiped down before painting, spraying, or staining. The grain of the wood often becomes prominent when stained, and looks well varnished.

Cleaning and Stripping

Always examine the existing paintwork thoroughly. Is it in a good condition? Bad paintwork must be stripped with a proprietary paint stripper.

After using the stripper as described earlier, the next job is to take a bucket of clean water and sponge down the body. Wash well into corners, for it is here that dirt and grease settle and prevent the paint from drying. Dry off with clean rags, then dry-rub down with abrasive paper.

Never leave bare metal exposed to the weather; it rusts up in a matter of a few hours. Look for rusty parts, and give these a coat of rust preventive mixture as mentioned earlier.

CHAPTER 3

MASKING AND REPAIRING DENTS

A spraying job can never look finished if dents are not repaired properly, and the best time to do this is before spraying on the priming coat. Bad dents should be dealt with by an expert panel beater, or repair body man.

Patience is needed when knocking out dents, but there is no reason why dents on the average car cannot be repaired by the sprayer. To knock out the imperfections use a wooden mallet and tap the dent out carefully from the underside. Hold a block of wood on the outside of the dent; this will help to steady the tapping out. Try to tap each dent out as level as possible. The care you take in doing this has a great effect on the finished job. Never leave part of a knocked-out dent above the level of the surrounding surface.

Having done this job deal immediately with any rust. Parts around and inside dents usually rust up. Remove the rust with a wire brush. Wipe the surface clean, then treat with a rust preventive mixture. This mixture is in liquid form and can be applied with an ordinary paint brush. Rust preventive mixture provides an excellent 'key' for the priming coat.

The next job is to touch in with a little priming the places where the dents have been, then fill up level with surrounding surface with car stopper, sometimes called knifing stopper. Use a painter's flexible scraper to press home the stopper and level off neatly with surrounding surface.

Small dents need not be knocked out. They can be wire brushed, treated with rust preventive mixture, and filled up in the usual way. Always allow a good 24 hours for the stopper to set, then rub down to surface level.

Rubbing down after dents have been filled up should be done with 'wet' abrasive paper. Begin rubbing with No. 280 paper, dip this in a bucket of warm soapy water and rub over the complete body until smooth. Afterwards give the whole car body a good washing down with clean cold water. It is most important at this stage to remove all dirt, oil or grease. If there is dirt on the underside of mudguards this can be blown on the new paint by the air stream from the spray gun.

The next job is to dry off the whole car body, go over it thoroughly with clean dry rags, then leave it to dry out thoroughly. This is most important.

Thinning Paint

When it is necessary to thin paint, correct thinners should be used. Cellulose thinners for cellulose; turps substitute for synthetic or oil paints; methylated spirits for shellac, French polish or spirit paints.

The amount of thinners to be used will vary according to circumstances. Overthinning should be avoided. Use only just enough thinners to make the material sprayable, to flow easily from the gun. Follow the manufacturers' instructions to the letter.

The material will not spray evenly if insufficient thinners is employed. When the pressure of the spray gun is low the material must be thinner. As a general guide about 30 per cent of thinners should be added; this can be increased a little as the work proceeds. Here again, follow the manufacturers' instructions. Keep a note of the quantity of thinners used; it will enable you to get the correct amount needed when preparing paint for future spraying.

Thinning and mixing of paint should be done to cover the complete job before beginning to spray. This will save thinning and mixing later. A primer needs little thinning, and care should be taken not to overthin the paint. This fault may cause runs and tend to spoil the work. Thinners for cellulose, synthetic, or oil-based materials should be purchased by the gallon. This will be found more economical.

When thinning synthetic materials use only those thinners supplied by the makers of the paint. Some difficulty may be experienced with spray paint in cold weather—it may not flow freely. One way to overcome this difficulty is to heat up the paint. Lightly ease the lid of the container and place it in a bucket of warm water. Sufficient material can be taken from the container from time to time as spraying proceeds, and the warm water can be replaced when necessary. Care should be taken to keep the water out of the paint and the spray gun.

Straining Paint

Avoid using dirty paint, for it clogs up the jet of the spray gun. If in doubt strain paint through a sieve, or an old nylon stocking. Fix this over the container and pour a little paint into it at a time. Gradually work it about with an old brush. The paint will pass through and the sediment will be left behind.

Masking Before Spraying

Certain parts on a car, such as headlamps, number-plates and windows have to be protected from off-spray, caused through atomisation.

Old newspapers are handy for this job. They can be fixed securely with adhesive tape. Brown paper is much better. It can be cut to the sizes required, it does not tear, and it can be secured with masking tape or paste.

Whenever possible it is best to remove fittings because they are liable to cause runs when you spray round them. When spraying wheels deflate tyres and push pieces of cardboard between the tyre rim and the tube. Afterwards inflate a little to keep in position. Masking paper may also be fixed with rubber solution; this makes the paper easy to remove.

Always secure paper or other protective material securely. Remember, there is always a certain amount of pressure from the spray gun, and this can remove insecure masking. A certain amount of paint may get under the masking, causing extra work when the job is finished.

Never spray more paint than is necessary on the masking material, for it may get under the edges and be difficult to remove. A coat of whitening brushed on glasswork gives a good protection. It can be easily wiped off when the job is finished.

Masking tape, masking paste and masking fluid can be purchased from all paint shops. The parts of the car which need masking are windows, windscreen and wheels.

When masking is difficult to remove sponge it with warm water and it will easily peel away. Should small amounts of paint get under the masking and adhere to the glasswork, remove with a little thinners and rag.

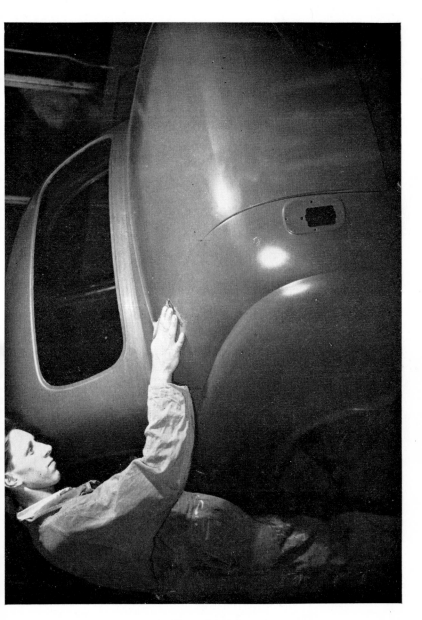

Rubbing down dry

Cleaning a Spray Gun after use

(Courtesy Farmer & Stockbreeder)

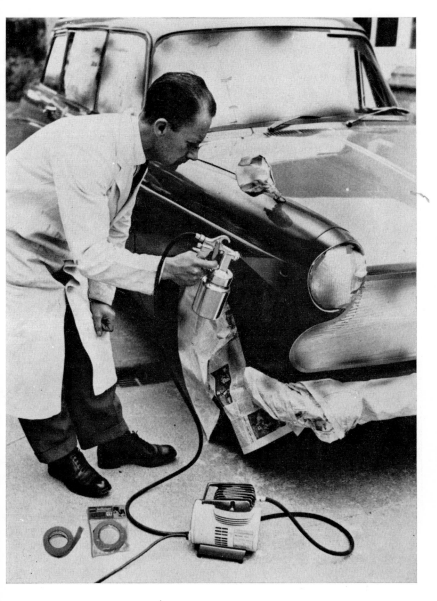

Spraying—notice how wheels, bumpers etc. are protected by paper

(*Courtesy Burgess Products & Co. Ltd., Leicester*)

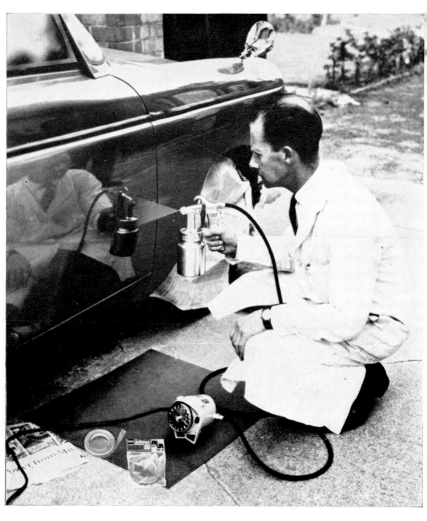

Spraying in Progress

(*Courtesy Burgess Products & Co. Ltd., Leicester*)

CHAPTER 4

THE RIGHT WAY TO SPRAY

Getting the Knack

If you have never used a spray gun before, it is advisable to get a little practice before beginning the actual job. Try the gun out on a spare wall, or on a spare petrol tin. This will give you confidence and help you to get the knack of trigger pressure, which is important.

The object of spraying is to apply an even wet coat of paint to the surface, near to the running state but never actually running. If the gun is moved too quickly across the surface the paint coat will be too thin; on the other hand if the gun is moved too slowly, the coating will be too thick, causing runs.

For good spraying one must acquire the happy medium—not too quick, not too slow. The fan-shaped spray pattern now provided by most guns is considered to be the best. The spray pattern can be adjusted, from a fan shape to a horizontal or vertical pattern.

Manufacturers of spray guns always issue instructions for operating their particular type of gun. The adjustment of several types of gun in amateur use is made from the nozzle adapter of the gun by discs or by a knob. The professional types of gun have removable spray heads; these suit both thin and thick materials.

Spray guns have different jet sizes. The smaller jet is used for thin materials, and the larger one for heavy materials. The main feature of modern spray guns is the needle valve. This can be regulated to control the amount of paint leaving the jet of the gun.

Correct Distance to Stand from Work

It is essential to hold the gun at the correct distance from the work. This may require a little practice. If the gun is held too far away, the paint will not reach the surface in a full wet coat. But if the gun is held too near, the air pressure will affect the paint film. The distribution of the paint will be poor and the coating will be uneven.

The correct distance to stand away when spraying is from 9 to 10 inches, and this should be kept continually in mind throughout the job.

Trigger Manipulation

Assuming that the car body is ready for the priming coat, stir up the paint and make certain it is free from bits of dirt. If in doubt strain it.

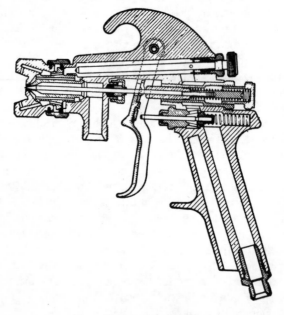

Modern Spray Gun

Always test the spray pattern for correct atomization and good shape. You can do this by spraying a piece of plain glass with finishing paint. Look at the glass from the reverse side and you will see any imperfections of the spray pattern. If it is unsatisfactory adjust the gun.

The art of spraying means developing a smooth, even stroke. This is called 'feathering out' at the beginning and end of each stroke.

Start to spray by pressing the trigger of the gun fully back. This enables you to hit the surface with a full spray. When possible hold the gun at right angles to the surface. Allow an overlap of half an inch per stroke to ensure good coverage. Begin each stroke as far to the left or right as possible. Pull the trigger gradually back when beginning a stroke, hold it fully back till the end of stroke then gradually release it. Then lower the gun and start another stroke in the opposite direction, to overlap the previous stroke.

Work slowly and the knack of trigger pressure will soon be achieved. Always avoid rapid, jerky strokes and aim to keep each stroke a steady, firm movement. Try to do the job with the least number of strokes.

Spray edges, recesses, window frames, fillets and mouldings round doors and fittings first, then finish off with the general bodywork.

Surfaces ending in corners should be sprayed to within one or two inches of the corner. Then spray the corner in such a way as to cover both the bare edges of the main surface at once.

A good light is always essential for the job; it helps one to avoid runs and misses and to judge the condition of the work. Fluorescent tubes are the best means of artificial lighting during Winter. If possible try to do your car spraying during the Spring and Summer months, for natural lighting is the best.

Number of Spray Coats

Primer (First Coat). Knock out dents before spraying. See Chapter 3.

After spraying on primer allow 12 hours to dry hard—this is important. Afterwards fill up dents, then lightly rub down and dust off.

Resurfacer Coats

After priming, spray on resurfacer coats. The quality of the paint build-up depends upon good resurfacing coats. Remember that a cellulose finish provides very little filling, and a scratch if not adequately filled will show on the finish. Always spray on sufficient resurfacer coats to get a sound foundation.

Mist Coat

This is the first coat of resurfacer. It should be sprayed on in a thin coat. Do not over-thin it; add 10 per cent of thinners to the material.

After the mist coat, spray on three or four coats of resurfacer at full strength. Allow three hours between each coat for drying. Sometimes wet spots appear; wipe these off with a clean rag. Avoid runs at all times, and spray on an extra coat of resurfacer if not satisfied. Remember, the object is to build up a good foundation.

Wet Rubbing and Finishing

When the resurfacer is nice and hard, wet-rub down as mentioned in Chapter 2. Use soapy water and wet abrasive paper to get the best results. A smooth surface is essential. When foreign matter accumulates during rubbing wash it off immediately.

Spraying the Finish

Make sure the surface is dry, and do the job on a warm day if possible or heat the garage to 75 degrees, to help the paint to dry. Do everything possible to avoid dust, which is the enemy of the sprayer. Give the surface a final wipe over with clean rags before spraying. Spray on a thin mist coat, allow 40 minutes to dry, then spray on a full first coat followed by a second coat when dry. Afterwards spray on a final coat of 75 per cent thinners, and 25 per cent cellulose. This should give a durable finish.

CHAPTER 5

DEALING WITH IMPERFECTIONS

Before polishing examine the work for defects such as runs or scratches.

Faults on a cellulose finish are not difficult to deal with. Runs are caused through spraying too much material in one place. Runs may occur on the resurfacer coat as well as on the finish; these should be put right before the finish is sprayed.

Cellulose dries very hard, and runs are easily put right. The run should be rubbed down level with the surrounding surface, and then sprayed over again with resurfacer. If the run is heavy it can be taken off with a razor blade. Cut the edge and it can be removed in thin strips. Wet-rub down the defect, dry off and spray on a resurfacer coat. If too much material is removed, two or more coats of resurfacer should be sprayed on till filled up. Finally rub down to feather edge and blend with surrounding surface. When a final finishing coat is sprayed the run should not be noticed.

Runs appearing on a cellulose finish should be rubbed down and be sprayed over with cellulose thinners. Then spray with two coats of cellulose at full strength. A touching-in pencil is very handy for filling and coating up scratches.

Synthetic Finish

Treating runs on a synthetic finish is more difficult. The work must be allowed 24 hours or more to dry. Wet-rub down the run and area around it until level with surrounding surface. Afterwards re-spray with resurfacer and, after this has dried, with finishing paint.

Synthetic materials dry more slowly than cellulose and the repairs take longer to do.

You can easily obtain touching-in colours from local garages or

Halfords. Touching-in colours are sold in ¼-pint tins with brush. One well-known brand is touch-in Belco. It is available in all modern car colours.

Always clean your spray gun after use in the correct solvent. Use cellulose thinners for cellulose, and turpentine substitute or white spirits for synthetic.

Polishing

A cellulose finish needs polishing. This gives it a flawless plate-glass appearance. Polishing should be done with soft linen rags.

There are many car polishes on the market today. Some are used as a cutting paste or mild abrasive. They should be used first followed by the final polish, which should be a good weather-resisting wax polish.

There is a knack in polishing. It can be done in a circular movement or in straight strokes. A cellulose finish is so hard that it can stand much rubbing without damage; it is not wise, however, to over-polish new paintwork. Do the job gradually.

Make the polishing cloth into a pad and see it is dry and clean. Go over the surface lightly yet firmly. Apply just sufficient polish to form a thin layer over the entire surface then rub evenly to polish. You may not be able to get that plate-glass finish immediately, but with patience you will get it in a matter of a week or two. Care should be taken not to over-polish one part and neglect another.

When the pad becomes clogged during polishing change it immediately. Many paint makers supply special car polish, which is not difficult to apply. A good wax polish is the best if your car is parked outside.

Spraying Faults

These are some of the most common faults when car spraying:

Popping. The temperature of the garage is higher than that of the surface of car. Heat should not be used for drying until paint is set.

Bridging. Mouldings are not cleaned out after rubbing down. This fault is also due to applying filter or resurfacer coats too thick. The remedy—wash out mouldings as clean as possible and avoid thick coats of paint; apply it in even coats.

Sags. These are due to a dirty air cap on the spray gun, which causes a distorted spray pattern; or the trouble may result from holding the gun too close to the surface. Remedy—remove the air cap and clean it, and stand 9 to 10 ins. from surfaces when spraying.

Other faults may be that the trigger of the gun was not released at the end of each stroke; or the gun was stroked at the wrong angle to the surface. Always release the trigger at the end of each stroke; always point the gun at right angles to the surface; avoid over-thinning paint.

Streaks on paint are caused by a dirty air cap on the gun, incorrect overlapping of strokes, gun strokes too rapidly, gun held too far from the surface, too much air pressure, or split spray through dirty material. Remedy—remove the air cap and clean the spray with level, steady strokes; use as little pressure as necessary.

Orange Peel. The paint was not thinned sufficiently, or there was too much air pressure. Remedy—add the correct amount of thinners by measure, check the thinners, and use the correct speed and overlap of strokes.

Excessive spray fog, or over-spray, is due to high air pressure. It is caused by spraying too far past the surface of the car, holding the gun too far from surface, or over-thinning the paint. The remedy— use less pressure, release the trigger when the gun passes the end of the surface, stroke the gun 9 to 10 ins. from the surface, and measure the correct amount of thinners.

Excessive paint loss is due to holding the gun too far away from the surface; or the air pressure was too high. Remedy—hold the gun at the correct distance, and use pressure with care.

When paint fails to come from the spray gun, the latter begins to splutter. Dirt or grit is blocking the fluid tip, air passage or nozzle.

Strain your paint before using, and clean your spray gun thoroughly.

When the gun splutters constantly, the nozzle is not tightened up correctly. The threads may be defective.

Paint leaking from gun. The fluid needle packing nut is too tight. Slack off and clean.

Blushing or *blooming* is caused by absorption of moisture from atmosphere. The remedy—use anti-chill thinners and inspect the gun for leaking parts.

Pinholing. There was oil or water in the water or the spray gun, or if cellulose, the paint was over-thinned. Remedy—clean the filters and strain the paint. Avoid excess heat—the correct temperature is 75 degrees. Thin the paint by correct measurement.

TABLE OF OPERATIONS WHEN SPRAYING

1. Remove the old finish.
2. Knock out dents and remove rust.
3. Wash down with clean soapy water.
4. Rub down with abrasive paper and wipe over with clean rags soaked in turps. substitute.
5. Spray on priming coat.
6. Stop up imperfections; rub down when hard.
7. Spray on mist coat of resurfacer.
8. Spray on full coats of resurfacer.
9. Give a complete wet rubbing down.
10. Spray on mist coat of cellulose, or synthetic.
11. Spray on further coats of finish.
12. Deal with imperfections, if any.
13. Polish.
14. Synthetic finishes can be given a coat of synthetic varnish, or be polished.

CHAPTER 6

For those who do not like spraying, brush painting is the alternative. Some excellent work can be done with the brush; the old coach-painters proved this.

Keeping Brushes

Buy your paint brushes from a reputable maker. Hamiltons are outstanding in this field. A good brush should have straight soft bristles with a kind of chisel shape at the end of the bristles.

Treat your brushes with care and respect. Thousands of paint brushes are ruined each year through neglect. They are used in paint until the job is finished, then carelessly placed aside with their bristles full of paint, which sets hard. Constant soaking in solvents fails to bring such brushes back to normal. One can never do a decent job with them again.

Always try to have a set of brushes for each colour. The range should include ¼- and ½-inch, 1-inch and 2-inch flat varnish brushes. One 3-inch is handy for large surfaces. A small sable writing pencil is handy for touching up.

When the painting job is finished always work the surplus paint out of your brushes. Do this on old newspapers or an old board. Brushes will keep soft in clear water, which should be changed periodically.

Always keep your brushes in a brush keeper, which can be made from an empty colour tin. Bore a ⅝-inch hole through the base of the handles, pass a steel rod through them and suspend them in clean water. This prevents the ends of the bristles from touching the bottom of the keeper and so being turned up and distorted.

It is unwise to suspend paint brushes in linseed oil or turpentine.

37.

Such a mixture causes dirt to be drawn up into the bristles by capillary action. This mixture is also difficult to remove from the bristles, and it tends to mix with the paint being used.

Brushes used in dark colours should be kept separate from those used in light colours. Brushes used only one or twice a year should be washed out in thinners, and then be given a final wash in warm soapy water.

To prepare an ideal varnish brush use it for a duster until the bristles become chisel shaped. This will make it ideal for laying off varnish. To get this shape quickly lay the brush on a smooth hard surface, spread the bristles out and cut off all projecting ones. Rub out any loose hairs on old newspapers.

'Polyclens' makes the cleaning of paint brushes easy. All you have to do is to rinse the bristles in the liquid, then wash them under the tap and all the paint washes out. This makes it possible to change from black to white paint immediately, using only one brush.

Brush Painting

Quite good work can be done by brush painting, especially on second-hand cars and vans.

If you are doing the job in a garage see that the place is absolutely clean beforehand. Remove all cobwebs from walls and ceiling and scrub the floor with warm water. Dirt and dust are the enemy of the painter. Heat the garage if the weather is cold to a temperature of 75 degrees to assist the paint in drying.

Brush painting is much the same as spray painting. The important thing is that paint must be applied to a good clean surface, as when spraying. It is useless to paint over a surface which needs stripping; you must begin with a good hard foundation so that the paint will grip.

Use a good paint remover and apply two or three coats, giving the stripper time to do its job—this is 10 to 15 minutes. Scrape old paint off with a painter's broad knife, and use a triangular scraper for removing paint from crevices and corners. Then knock out dents as described in Chapter 3. Next give the surface a good dry rubbing down to remove dirt or foreign matter. Keep a look-out for rust. This should be rubbed off with a wire brush, and the parts should be given a coat of rust preventative mixture. Finally wipe the whole body well over with rags soaked in turpentine substitute or petrol, and fill up dents as described in Chapter 3.

The Priming Coat

The first coat of paint should now be brushed on. Stir the paint well. Dip only the ends of the bristles into the material and brush it over the surface in a thin coat. Work the paint well into corners and crevices, covering mouldings and around fittings first, then finish off with flat surfaces.

In brush painting the main thing to remember is to work the paint well about and rub it well in, and put on just enough to cover. Brush up and down, then brush crosswise, and finally lay off with light strokes. Never put too much paint on the surface—a common fault of amateur car painters. Load the brush lightly and distribute evenly. Overloading the brush means a thick coat of paint which causes runs and congeals on the edges; it seldom dries hard and causes cracking and blisters. A thin coat well brushed about is what is needed; this dries hard and gives a firm foundation for the next coat. Allow priming 24 hours to dry hard.

Resurfacer Coat

Next wipe the surface with clean rags and apply a thin coat of re-surfacer (undercoat), and when sufficiently hard apply two more coats at normal strength. Allow about 12 hours between each coat for drying off. The object of the resurfacer as in spraying is to get a build-up foundation for the finishing coat. Take extreme care in applying the resurfacer coats. Stir the paint well and apply a good level coating free from runs.

Wet Rubbing

Use soapy water as a lubricant and rub the surface with wet abrasive paper. Use a coarse paper at the beginning and finish off with a smooth paper. One important point to remember, as mentioned in Chapter 2, is to keep the fingers holding abrasive together, to ensure even pressure throughout the operation. Avoid misses and be sure to rub over the whole surface. Afterwards wash down with clean water and wipe dry.

Brushing on the Finish

The finishing material should be a hard gloss finishing weather-resisting paint or enamel. There are many types of coach finishes on the market, both synthetic paints and enamels. It is not safe to intermix these unless purchased from the same firm. Buy your materials—primer, undercoat and finishing—from a firm of repute, and you will get good materials.

There is a tendency for all finishing paints to work stiff under the brush. This means that they must be well brushed out, otherwise you will get runs which tend to spoil the job. It is quite easy to put on too much material. This can only be avoided by good distribution of the paint, as pointed out in application of priming. All material must be laid off lightly with upward strokes to get a plate-glass finish.

Avoid putting on the finishing coat in dull cold weather. Do the job on a sunny day if possible. Cold and damp make the paint lose its gloss.

Although there is a brushing cellulose which would have to be polished, synthetic materials are much better and simpler for brush painting. These are manufactured from selected synthetic resins and top-quality pigments. They possess high gloss and excellent build up, and need little polishing.

Touching Up. Dealing With Abrasions

Most second-hand cars were originally finished in cellulose. Even when aged, cellulose may lift a new coat of synthetic paint placed over it. To be on the safe side give the whole surface a good coat of sealer before repainting, provided the surface is good.

No priming coat is needed. After sealer apply undercoat. Stop up if necessary, wet-rub down and apply the finishing coat. In some cases when the old paintwork is in good condition no resurfacer or undercoat is needed. Wet-rub the surface down and give a coat of sealer if necessary; when dry follow on with finishing coat. Sometimes one coat of finishing paint will be sufficient. 'Half-hour enamel', made by Lewis Berger, is suitable for a quick one-coat repaint during the week-end.

Abrasions

Paint on mudguards often gets chipped, exposing the bare metal. To repair these defects dry-rub down with glasspaper and touch in with priming. When sufficiently hard apply two coats of resurfacer, and when dry feather out edges of repair by wet rubbing. Finally coat with finishing paint.

Matching colours can be had at all stockists such as Halfords. In some cases it is best to give the mudguards a full coat of finishing paint.

Materials required for repainting a 10 h.p. van by brush:

¼ gallon synthetic grey primer.
¼ gallon undercoat or resurfacer.
¼ gallon hard weather-resisting enamel, or gloss paint.
1 lb. stopper.
10 sheets wet and dry abrasive paper.

You will of course require supplies of paint stripper and some rust preventative mixture if the van is in a poor condition. It will take about 40 hours spread over 5 days for a good job. The time could be longer or shorter: this depends upon the condition of the van.

CHAPTER 7

REPAINTING ON WOOD

BOX WOOD VANS

GRAINING, VARNISHING AND FRENCH POLISHING

Painting on wood is to some extent different from painting on metal, but it can be quite interesting. For instance, owners of box wood vans, shooting brakes, etc., can give their vehicles a superior finish by painting, simple graining and varnishing.

Old paintwork on wood often through the passage of time, and wear and tear, blisters and peels away. This must be removed before painting The best way to do this is with a blow lamp. The heat from the lamp does the surface a great deal of good. It helps to fill up the grain of the wood, and this prevents moisture entering.

A paraffin blow lamp is the most suitable for the job, but care should be taken when using this. The usual blow lamp works upon the combustion principle, and should be started as follows. Saturate a piece of cotton wool with paraffin, then place it in the well of the lamp, and light it. Keep the lamp away from draughts and it will gradually warm up. This takes a few minutes. Close the air valve on the side, then gradually pump air into the lamp.

The air pressure from pumping makes the nipple emit a blue flame with a roaring sound. Pump sufficient air into the lamp till enough power is obtained, and close the air valve on the side before pumping. Should the nipple become clogged through dirt insert the pricker provided with the lamp into it; this puts out the flame but it can be lighted immediately by holding a lighted match to it.

Burning Off

Play the flame only a few seconds in one place. When the paint blisters and softens up push it off with a painter's broad scraper. Avoid playing the flame of the lamp in one place too long, for this scorches the woodwork. Burn off edges first and flat surfaces last, using the triangular scraper to remove paint from mouldings and corners. When the job is completed wrap a piece of dry abrasive paper over a 4-inch block of wood, then give the whole surface a vigorous dry rubbing down. Dust off and wipe clean.

Rubbing down often reveals knots. Give these a coat of shellac, or French polish. This dries rapidly and seals up the knots, preventing moisture from entering.

All woodwork when plain painted should have at least three good coats of paint—priming, undercoat and finishing.

The first coat, lead priming, gives good protection, and is generally a mixture of white lead paint to which a little red lead has been added. This lead coat needs brushing on thinly after well stirring, and should be left for a day or so to dry.

The next job is to stop up with putty, and to rub down lightly with dry glasspaper and dust off. Afterwards follow on with undercoat, dry-rub this down, wipe clean, and apply the gloss finish. Use a warm place for applying the finishing coat, or do the work on a dry, warm day.

A superior finish may be obtained by applying two coats of buff undercoating over the priming. If a light oak finish is required apply a light buff coat; if a dark oak finish apply a dark buff colour. This provides the groundwork on which to do simple brush graining.

Simple Graining

Simple graining is not difficult. Simple brush and comb graining can be done quite easily. It gives quite a superior finish to woodwork, especially on box wood vans.

The object of graining is to imitate or copy the natural colour and grain of the various hardwoods such as oak. After preparation and painting of the buff groundwork, the job is ready for staining. This is done with scumble oil graining colour.

Mix up the stain to the consistency of cream, dilute it with turps substitute, then try out a little on a spare board. If it is too thin it will run; if too thick it will dry out patchy. A little practice will give you some idea of how the stain should be brushed out.

Use a stiff brush and stain edges first and large surfaces last. Try to stain one part completely before beginning another part. Rub in the stain as quickly as possible and dry brush out evenly, then while the stain is wet draw a stiff dry brush down the work in a straight or wavy line to imitate the plain grain of oak.

For comb graining take a broad graining steel comb, begin at the right edges of the work and draw it down the work till half is completed. Next take a fine comb and begin on the other side of the work and join up to the broad combing. This looks well on a panel. The combing can be done in straight or wavy strokes.

The more ambitious may like to try figure graining. Examination of real oak reveals a plain grain running lengthwise and the figure crossing it. The plain grain is put in with a stiff dry brush and steel combs, as pointed out. Rub the stain into the surface in the usual way, then after brushing and combing put in the figuring. Do this with a piece of soft rubber cut to a chisel point. Afterwards parts of the stain are wiped out to make rays, veins, rings and heart growth. Afterwards a soft brush is drawn over the work to give a feathering-out effect. This work can only be achieved with practice.

Overgraining

Simple brush and comb graining can be made to look superior when overgrained. The enterprising amateur taking pains can achieve this effect.

Rub the work over with a lightly damped sponge rubbed in powdered whitening; this prevents the overgraining from working up in small beads called scissing. Next take very thin stain and lightly paint in veins, rings and rays with a soft lead pencil. When the panel is completed feather out the whole by drawing a soft brush over the work. It is essential to give all grained work a coat of good hard weather-resisting varnish.

Graining Tools and Mechanical Graining

A set of rubber graining tools makes it possible to grain by mechanical means. Having prepared and stained the surface select the tool required. The corrugated or heart tools make a coarse grain or best heart growths; the veined tools produce finer grains and champs; or the quartered oak tool with comb and blender may be used.

A straight grain is made by simply drawing the tool down the surface of the work. A heart growth is obtained by rocking the tool back and forth as drawn along. Reversed grains may be made by running the tool off the panel and starting again at the opposite end.

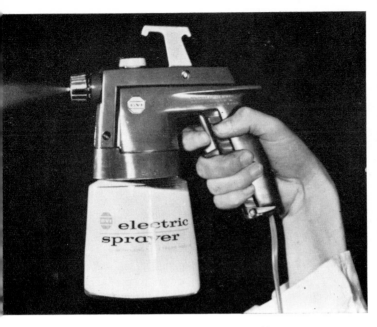

Suitable Spray Gun for the "Do it Yourself Man"
(*Courtesy Burgess Products & Co. Ltd., Leicester*)

Another Spray Gun
(*Courtesy Alfred Bellows & Sons Ltd., Walsall*)

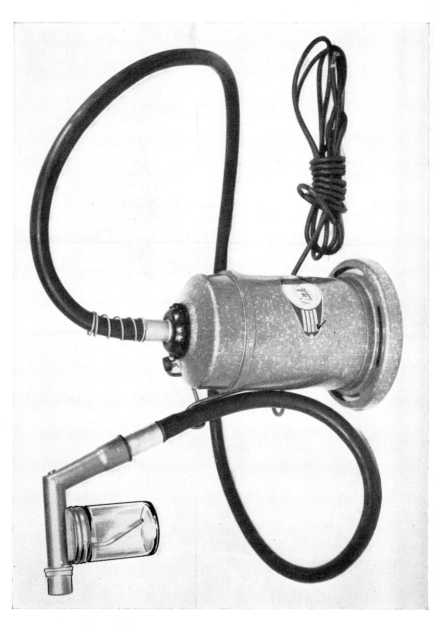

The Bylock Vortex Mark 11 low pressure Spraying Unit

(Courtesy Bylock Electrical Ltd., Enfield)

The Cyclone Spraying Unit Mark IV

(Courtesy Bylock Electrical Ltd., Enfield)

Modern High Pressure Spray Gun

It is claimed that no two grains are exactly alike. It is essential, however, to bear firmly on the surface when working the grainers to ensure correct impression. The grainers are able to grain both convex and concave surfaces. These graining tools are made by the Ridgely Trimmer Co., 117 Clerkenwell Road, London, E.C.1.

The Right Way to Varnish

Before the introduction of cellulose enamels and spray painting the technique of varnishing achieved a high standard. Varnish can give a very superior finish to all grained work and renew the life of all painted work.

Varnish is a delicate substance, so all work should be done in absolutely clean surroundings. A cold atmosphere makes the material lose its lustre. Never keep a varnish brush in water; it is detrimental to varnish, causing it to go dull.

There are today about 300 different types of varnish on the market. The two main types are oil and synthetic.

Manufacturers now produce special coach varnishes suitable for cars or vans. They produce a high degree of gloss and weather resistance. If possible avoid thinning varnish. It leaves the factory at the correct brushing consistency in airtight containers. It only becomes thick if exposed to the air for long periods. If this happens it may be thinned by gently heating in a bucket of warm water.

Use varnish direct from the container, and seal this up immediately the job is finished. It is essential to flat or dull a glossy surface before varnishing. Do this with soapy water and wet abrasive paper, and before applying the varnish thoroughly dry off the surface.

Application

The varnish must be distributed without runs. When beginning a job examine the surface to determine where to begin and finish. This will give you some idea where interruptions will occur. Varnish flows out to a level surface if brushed on evenly and carefully. Varnish the panels first and work round the vehicle, finishing at the bonnet.

When laying on the varnish go round doors, edges, and all less important parts first, leaving the main bodywork till last. Always use a small brush to varnish corners and edges, and cover the main panels last. The brush should be fairly well charged and applied to the top of the surface, then drawn down in a vertical direction. Increase the pressure on the brush as the varnish is used up. Lay the next stroke alongside the first stroke and blend the varnish with that already applied, as when using paint.

Do one section at a time, increasing pressure on the brush till the material is used up, gently brushing and finally laying the work off with light upwards strokes. Opinion differs as to the amount of varnish to be laid on the surface. It is better to put on too much than too little, then gradually work it off again. In my opinion only just that amount necessary should be left on the surface; remember there is always the danger of runs to spoil the work. Should these occur stipple them out with a dry brush.

Hardwoods like oak may be finished satisfactorily by varnishing, provided the wood is filled up. Proprietary fillers can be used but a good filler can be made by mixing together powdered French chalk with equal parts of turpentine and goldsize.

Use this in a thin paste and rub it into the grain of the wood crosswise to the grain with clean rags. Other possible fillers are plaster of Paris and pumice powder. They can be mixed with a little stain to match the colour of the wood.

When the filler sets rub down with glasspaper and lightly stain if necessary. Afterwards apply a coat of hard-wearing synthetic varnish thinned with 10 per cent turpentine, to act as a primer. Allow ample time to dry, then rub down with glasspaper, dust off, and apply a coat of varnish at full strength. To get a very high-gloss surface apply more coats of varnish. Flat down each coat by lightly rubbing with glasspaper before applying the final coat of varnish.

Defects in Varnish

Varnish may go 'seedy' or 'bitty', giving the appearance of having been sprinkled with fine sand. This is caused through storing varnish in a cold place. Dirt in the varnish brush may also cause this.

Bad preparation of the surface or uneven application makes varnish 'sag' or 'shrivel'. Varnish exposed to cold draughts, or overthinned with turpentine, may also be responsible for this defect.

When the atmosphere is charged with moisture, varnish may dry in pinholes or appear blotchy. Mixing two different kinds of varnish from different makers together will also cause this; so will varnishing over a surface not properly dry.

When varnish sinks into the surface it is a sign that the surface was not properly prepared, not well primed or filled. When varnish peels or cracks, sufficient time has not been allowed for the paintwork to dry before varnishing. When the material becomes dull, with a whitish appearance, damp or cold is the cause. A clean warm surface is most essential for good varnishing.

Staining

Two main types in use today are oil stains and spirit stains. The latter are used for quick jobs. Apart from oil stain like scumble, used for graining, black japan is very useful. It can be diluted with turpentine to make a light or dark oak stain.

The woodwork of shooting brakes and similar vehicles can be easily stained, provided the stain is well protected with varnish. Proprietary oil stain is supplied in most natural wood colours; it needs only diluting with turps.

Hardwoods as a rule require little staining, but plywood can be effective when stained; the grain of the wood can be brought into prominence. All that is needed is a little skill. A good way to get an effect is to have a dipper of equal parts of goldsize and turps handy. Rub this into the surface, then dip a corner of the rag into some thick stain, and with light touches darken where necessary. The lines and turns in the grain of the wood can be followed.

A little touch here and there makes all the difference. A knot, a broad sweep and a curl may be introduced. Common woods can be made to look like expensive ones when varnished.

Easy Way of French Polishing

Certain parts of woodwork on the interior of cars or caravans look well if French-polished. This often helps one to get rid of stains and blemishes. The work is not difficult to do, as is sometimes imagined; in fact it is quite easy and interesting.

The materials are not expensive—one pint of French polish, some methylated spirits, a little raw linseed oil, medium glasspaper, clean rag and cotton wool are all that is needed.

When the old polish is bad, remove it with a paint stripper, but most work can be prepared for polishing if you give it a good rubbing down then wipe it clean with methylated spirits.

You will need a polisher's rubber. To make this take a piece of clean cotton wool about the size of the hand, and press together to form a pad. Next soak it in the polish and wrap it in a piece of clean linen rag to complete the rubber. The flow of polish on the work is regulated by the pressure of the fingers on the rubber.

Begin by going over the work with light circular strokes overlapping each other. After applying a few coats allow the surface to dry thoroughly. This takes only five minutes. After each coat of polish is dry lightly rub over the surface with fine glasspaper. Keep repeating this process between each coat of polish. After a time the surface should take on a high gloss.

Avoid putting too much polish on the surface at one time, for this often causes the surface to become rough. Should this happen, lightly glasspaper, dust off and apply more polish.

Spiriting Off

Having obtained a glossy surface we now come to the job of spiriting off. This is the main part of the work. Pour two or three drops of methylated spirits on to the rubber and go over the work lightly and quickly. Do not let the rubber rest on the work—keep it moving and use only a little spirit to moisten the rubber.

The object of French polishing is to let the spirits take the place of the polish. After a time the surface should begin to take on a plate-glass look, and in the process of lightly rubbing with spirits will harden off. After a time use a new rubber with spirits only, then finish off by rubbing with a clean soft rag the way of the grain.

To do successful French polishing always work in a temperature of about 75 degrees. A damp cold atmosphere causes the work to go dull. Should this happen place the job aside for a time and the natural gloss will return.

The main faults to avoid are: applying too much polish, applying too much spirits, and working in a cold atmosphere. Good results may be obtained by using a soft brush to apply polish, then finishing with the rubber. To eliminate deep scratches or bad stains place a warm cloth over the defects and leave for a time. The heat causes the grain to swell and fill up the scratches. Afterwards glasspaper down and polish in the normal way.

CHAPTER 8

SIMPLE LINING, LETTERS, NUMERALS
AND STENCILLING

Few people can paint a line on a car body at the first attempt. One gets to know by touch and eyesight the correct pressure to put on lining brush. To become a free-hand liner needs some practice.

The lining colour should be a quick-drying synthetic enamel well stirred to give good coverage. A good lining pencil is essential and brown sable or pure sable hair are the most suitable. It is a good idea to fill up the ends of the pencil quill with a small piece of wood to serve as a handle. This makes it much better to handle the pencil when turning curves.

It is advisable to get in a little practice before attempting the actual job. Paint a piece of metal or board as for lining. Then take a piece of thread, chalk it and strike a chalked line where the proper line is to go. Next place a little colour on your palette and work it into the pencil without overcharging it.

Hold the pencil between the forefinger and thumb with the second and third fingers resting on the work and the body in a comfortable position. This should allow the elbow to work freely along the side of the body.

Place the liner in position on the chalk line and press down about two thirds, then draw the pencil along using a finger as a guide. Keep the pencil true on the chalk line and keep the same pressure throughout the stroke, to ensure equal thickness of the line. When the line shows signs of thinning recharge the pencil with colour.

As the colour dries the heel of the pencil is liable to become clogged and must be washed out in turpentine. Keep a dipper of turps handy for this and always use a clean palette.

Aids to Lining

If you are unable to do free-hand lining you need not despair. Try doing it with the aid of masking tape. Mark out with chalk where the line is to go, then fix two strips of masking tape parallel to each other. Allow a space of ⅛ inch or more between tapes to give depth of line.

Spray or paint between tapes. When paint is applied by brush lay it on level to give an even line. If you apply it too thin you will get ragged edges.

Immediately the work is finished peel away the masking tape. Never leave it till the paint dries; it will be difficult to remove then. With care and patience masking tape can be a very useful aid to lining.

The Rolls Paint Liner

For those who wish to undertake car spraying and painting in their spare time this lining tool is very handy. It is as easy to use as a pencil when you get the knack of it.

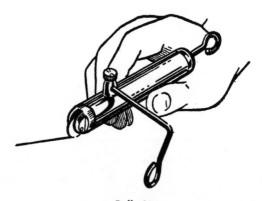

Rolls Liner

For good clean lines the paint must be of a creamy consistency. Flat paint or cellulose gives the best results. The lining tool is operated as follows: Remove the head, pull the plunger back and fill the barrel with as much paint as required. Select the head required and place it in the barrel with the wheel in line with the guide post. Then hold the liner with the head end up and push the plunger till paint appears at wheel. The liner is now ready for use.

The guide can be set to the required position by the guide adjusting screw. The lining tool is designed to be pulled across the surface. The wheel must revolve into the V of the head. This ensures that surplus paint is drawn back into the barrel.

The liner should be cleaned immediately after use, by removing the head and washing in petrol or thinners. The paint is pushed out of the barrel with the plunger. To clean the barrel work the plunger up and down, using thinners.

The main advantage of this lining tool is the positive feed of paint to the wheel. This enables it to be used in any desired position, on a flat surface, or even upside down. It makes parallel lines, straight lines, curves or circles in all paints, and on all types of surfaces, including metal, wood, or glass. The price of this liner is 27/-. It is sold with three heads, 1, 3/32 and 1/8-inch lines.

Simple Letters and Numerals

Although the painted number plate is quickly disappearing from cars, the plates of heavy vehicles and motor cycles are still hand painted. It is useful to be able to paint simple letters.

The chief requirements are a steady hand and some good taste. In all lettering a free and easy method of working is needed. This may not come at once, being to a great extent a matter of practice; some people have a natural flair for letters, others can achieve it with practice.

The best type of brush for lettering is a pure red sable known as a writing brush. These are sold according to their numbers; No. 1 is the smallest and No. 10 the largest. Writing pencils can be purchased at any artist's colourman.

Pure red sable pencils are very pliable and are undoubtedly the best for lettering. The mahl stick used by professional signwriters is the best means for steadying the hand, but it is not necessary for the amateur. The hand can be steadied by resting it on a book or resting it on the left hand laid flat. This is a matter of choice.

Practise a few brush strokes until you get familiar with the pencil. Do not hold the pencil too close to the hairs, and always rest the forefinger on the pencil. This enables you to roll the handle of the pencil slightly when making a curve. The edge of the pencil is kept down on the surface, making it possible to complete the curve almost in one sweep.

All number plates have block letters and numerals, and it is a good idea to study the complete block alphabet to get to know the actual shapes of the letters. The numerals from 0 to 9 should be studied also.

All letters and numerals should be written between two chalk lines, one at the top and one at the foot of the number plate. The best way to make these lines is to 'snap' them with a piece of thread. This is done as follows: take a piece of thread a little longer than the surface and tie an inch loop in the middle of it. Chalk the whole thread and holding an end in each hand stretch it tightly across the surface. When it is in the correct position take hold of the loop with the teeth, lift the line about an inch from the work and release it. It will snap back and leave a fine chalk line. Next, outline the letters or numerals with a piece of pointed chalk, and when painting in work dead on the lines.

It will be found that for lettering or numerals to be balanced, it is very necessary to vary the space occupied by certain letters. Curved letters or numerals should occupy more space than square letters. M requires about the thickness of its own stroke, more than N or H. O, C and Q are slightly wider than N, H and W. A double letter like W is wider at the top, leaving a space at the bottom on which an adjoining letter may encroach.

The whole object of spacing is for the letters to look evenly spaced, whereas in fact they are not. Practice will soon show which letters and numerals should be left a little larger. Note that all horizontal lines in the block alphabet appear thicker than they really are, and should be painted thinner.

All letters and numerals suitable for a car plate can be drawn in an oblong or square. It is a good idea to mark out the letters each in an oblong to ensure balance. This can be dispensed with when the shapes are familiar. Letters and numerals should be outlined first, then filled in later. They should have two coats of paint, a flat coat and a gloss coat. Wash the writing pencil in thinners after use and rub lanolin into the hair.

Stencilling

The making and using of stencils is a very useful craft to the handyman. Stencilling may be defined as the duplication or transference of a pattern to a surface by brushing colour through perforations cut in paper, cardboard, metal or other material.

Never look upon stencilling as a mechanical substitute for craft. Although stencilling has its limitations it can be put to practical use in lettering and designs.

Stencils can be divided into two classes, those in which ties are used to hold together the stencil, and those without ties. Those with ties are the most suitable for the handyman.

After stencilling is completed the ties can be filled in with a pencil brush.

How to Make a Stencil

The best material for making a stencil is cartridge paper, Whatman's drawing paper, or Manila paper. Japanese vellum is both tough and light. Stencilling paper can be purchased in rolls or sheets; special wax stencil paper is also available at artists' colourmen shops.

Before attempting to cut the paper soak it in raw linseed oil, or coat it with shellac varnish. The latter is the best and it dries quickly. This stiffens up the paper and makes it better for cutting.

Draw out the figures or letters required on white lining or transparent paper, then trace them on to the stencil paper, using a hard pointed pencil. For cutting the stencil a sharp knife is needed. A shoemaker's knife, called a 'clicker's knife', is ideal, but a sharp small penknife will do.

A good deal of pressure is required when cutting, and the job should be done on a hard, smooth surface, such as a sheet of plate glass or smooth metal.

When stencil paper is purchased in a roll it should be flattened out before cutting. This is done by rolling the paper in the opposite direction, or by drawing it over the edge of a table in a backward direction, holding the roll firmly.

Having got the paper into position, try to cut through it in one stroke. Cut out one section at a time, leaving in the ties. Cut across all projecting points and *away* from corners. You may spoil the first pattern through lack of practice, but a little patience will bring success. It is essential to hold the stencil firmly when cutting.

Stencilling

We now come to the actual stencilling. Hold the stencil flat and firmly down on the surface. Use a proper stencil brush and thick paint. Lightly charge the brush and draw it over a piece of clean cardboard to remove surplus paint. Apply the paint to the stencil in thick, short jabs, till the perforations are filled in. Avoid using too much paint on the brush; this causes it to creep under the stencil. When no stencil brush is available a small sponge is a good substitute.

Having filled in the stencil remove it carefully from the work to avoid smudges. Avoid using paint too thin, and always wipe clean the backs of stencils before beginning a fresh job. If you wish to get a two-coloured effect use two stencil brushes. Apply a light colour first then follow on with a dark colour; this enables two colours to be merged into one.

Spacing

The spacing at first may be a little difficult. It is a good idea to arrange the letters and numerals of a car plate before beginning the actual job. Strike a chalk line on the bottom edge of the plate and place the stencils along this. This will show you how they should fit in, and the chalk line will keep the stencilling straight.

Stencilling can be done by spray, provided adjoining surfaces are well masked. This is useful when duplicated work is required. Special stencil outfits with instructions can be purchased from artists' colour-men. These include cutting knives, ruler, colours in tubes, thinners and palette. As with other interesting jobs stencilling needs a little practice but it is rewarding. Once you have cut your car number plate you will always have it by you when repainting.

CHAPTER 9

GIVING THE INSIDE A NEW LOOK
LOOKING AFTER YOUR CAR
COLOURS

Often one observes a glittering new finish on the exterior of a car but immediately the door is opened a shabby interior is revealed. This looks even more drab when compared with the good exterior finish.

To begin with, mats and anything detachable should be removed, and then the whole interior should be gone over with a vacuum cleaner, the aim being to remove every particle of dirt.

After a time the roof lining of a car gets dirty. A good cleaning with tetrachloride will give it a new look. Afterwards give the head lining a good brushing with a dry brush. To clean upholstered rexine or real leather mix a good detergent in warm water to a stiff lather. When using this avoid flooding the leather work. Rub on the mixture thoroughly, then rinse off. A plastic sponge is useful, and the process of rinsing should be repeated twice or more until clean.

Many proprietary preparations are on the market, suitable for treating rexine or leather, and they can be applied by brush or spray. The interior of a car can be greatly improved by the use of these materials; they are made in various colours.

Quite a satisfactory job of leather or artificial leather can be made if sprayed with a mixture of linseed oil and cellulose. This should be mixed to the proportions of three of cellulose to one of linseed oil; the mixture dries fairly quickly and is flexible.

A shabby dashboard spoils a car. It can be cleaned and touched up by spray at intervals with cellulose or synthetic paint. The interior of windscreens and window frames is often chromium plated. This can be cleaned up with a mixture of powdered chalk and pure turpentine. Rub on, leave to dry, then wipe off and polish with a clean dry rag.

Tyre paint is a useful material when used on matting or the running boards, and on interior rubber mats. Liquid detergents are useful for cleaning carpets. One part of detergent to six parts of hot water is a good mixture. It should be used generously; afterwards the carpets can be hung up to dry, and their appearance will be greatly improved. Blinds frequently become dirty. They should be washed and ironed at intervals. After cleaning it is advisable to leave the car doors open, to dry.

A good material for cleaning all glasswork is methylated spirits. Give the surface a liberal application, then wipe off and polish with a clean rag. The polished woodwork of interior panels can also be touched up with methylated spirits; use this sparingly and finish off with a clean rag.

With care and patience you can make the interior of an old car very presentable, even equal to that of a new car.

Colours

Nowadays colours are purchased ready mixed, and each manufacturer has a special formula for making his own. Mixing colours made by two different manufacturers together is always risky. Mix colours together only if they were made by the same manufacturer. As pointed out previously, cellulose will not mix with synthetic or oil paint, and synthetic and oil paint should be mixed only with synthetic and oil.

For those who wish to do so, many shades of colours can be made by intermixing, using a white base paint or enamel. Some paint makers supply tubes of tinting colours for this purpose; these are useful when touching up and matching. Colours such as Prussian Blue, Crimson Red, Maroon and Deep Red should not be used for pastel shades, for they are liable to fade on exposure.

Red, Yellow and Blue are primary colours and cannot be made by intermixing other colours. Secondary colours are Green, Orange and Violet; they are composed of Blue and Yellow, Red and Yellow, and Blue and Red respectively. By mixing together two secondary colours we get what is called tertiaries—an unlimited series of tints.

The following list is useful for general colour mixing:

APRICOT. Mix together Orange and Green in equal parts.

BLUE AZURE. Base White, Prussian Blue.

BLUE GREY. Base White, Blue Black, a little Prussian Blue.

BROWN MISMARK. Base White, Burnt Sienna, Yellow, Burnt Umber.

BUFF COLOUR. Base White, Yellow Ochre.

CHOCOLATE. Venetian Red and Black.

CITRON. Base White, Chrome Yellow, a little Venetian Red.

CLARET. A little Ultramarine Blue, Venetian Red and Black.

CREAM. Base White, Chrome Yellow, a little Venetian Red.

CRIMSON. Dark Red, a little Carmine.

DOVE COLOUR. Base White, Lamp-black, Ultramarine Blue, a little Red.

DRAB COLOUR. Base White, Yellow Ochre, Burnt Umber.

FAWN. Base White, Stone Ochre, Vermilion.

FLESH PINK. Base White, a little Vermilion.

FRENCH GREY. Base White, Ivory Black.

IMITATION GOLD. Base White, Chrome Yellow, Burnt Sienna.

APPLE GREEN. Base White, Orange, Chrome Yellow, Prussian Blue.

BOTTLE GREEN. Prussian Blue, a little Lemon Chrome, a little Lamp Black.

GRASS GREEN. Base White, Ultramarine Blue, Chrome Yellow.

GREENS. Many other varieties can be made by mixing together Blue, Yellow and Black.

GREY, LIGHT. Base White, a little Lamp Black.

GREY PEARL. Base White, a small quantity of Lamp Black and Prussian Blue.

GREY STONE. Base White, a little Black and Yellow Ochre.

HELIOTROPE. Base White, Carmine, a little Orange, Chrome Yellow, Ivory Black.

KHAKI. Base White, Vermilion, Stone Ochre.

LEAD COLOUR. Base White and Lamp Black.

LEATHER. French Yellow, Burnt Umber, Venetian Red.

LIGHT OAK. Base White, Venetian Red, French Ochre.

LIGHT STONE. Base White, a little Venetian Red, Raw Umber.

MAHOGANY. Base White, a little Black, Venetian Red.

MAROON. Carmine Red, Ivory Black, a little Orange Chrome.

MAUVE. Venetian Red, Yellow Ochre, Lamp Black, a little White.

NUT BROWN. Base White, Light Red, Indigo Blue.

OLIVE BROWN. Four parts Lemon Yellow, eight parts Burnt Umber.

PEACH BLOSSOM. Base White, Prussian Blue, Chrome Yellow, Red.

PEACOCK BLUE. Base White, Cobalt Blue, a little Chinese Blue.

PORTLAND STONE. Base White, Yellow Ochre, Raw Umber.

RED SIGNAL. Base White, Venetian Red, Red Lead.

ROSE COLOUR. Pure Zinc White and Carmine Red.

RUSSET. Base White, Raw Umber, Chrome Green, a little Chrome Yellow.

SAPPHIRE BLUE. Base White and Chinese Blue.

SEAL BROWN. Medium Chrome Yellow, Base White and Burnt Umber.

SHELL PINK. Terra-Cotta paint, Pink paint.

SILVER GREY. Base White, Raw Umber, Ultramarine Blue, Lamp Black.

STONE COLOUR. Base White, Burnt Umber, Medium Chrome Yellow.

TURQUOISE. Base White, a little Green, Prussian Blue.

WALNUT. White Lead, Vermilion, a little Black and Blue.

Points Worth Noting when Colour Mixing

For Ivories and Creams, use Base White Colour; tint with Ochre, Black and Burnt Sienna.

For Greys, use Base Colours, Black and White; tint with Ochre, Oxide, Burnt Sienna and Blue.

Red tone Greys may be obtained with Black and Red Oxide. When a clean toned Red Grey is required, use Deep Purple Blue.

Green toned Greys require a little Black and Ochre. Blue Greys may require either Blue Black, or Black and Blue.

Blue deep shades. Base Colour Prussian Blue. Tint with Black and White.

Pastel Shades. Base Colours, White, Blue, Purple, Green and Red; tint with White, Black, Stone, Oxide or Cream.

Countless colours can be made by experimenting, and this can be a fascinating subject. Base White is the foundation for many attractive pastel shades when tinted with other colours.

Always mix your colours in good daylight and use the minimum of colours possible. Ensure that all sprayout of the mixture is quite dry before comparing it with the paint on the car being matched. Reds or maroons should be applied over a maroon gunglaze to assist the capacity. When you are matching part of a car it should be polished with a smoothing compound before you compare colours.

LIST OF MODERN COLOURS

Made by Berger for car finishing

These can be intermixed, but should be used with their primer and undercoats

AUSTIN RANGE			
Tweed Grey	4D.474	Balmoral Blue	4D.396
Chelsea Grey	4D.477	Streamline Blue	4D.475
Seal Grey	4D.391	Island Blue	4D.727
Court Grey	4D.725	Speedwell Blue	4D.792
Farina Grey	4D.1133	Kingfisher Blue	4D.812
Grampian Grey	4D.901	Ocean Blue	4D.916
Westminster Green	4D.389	Horizon Blue	4D.905
Spruce Green	4D.813	Orchid	4D.948
Palm Green	4D.793	Tartan Red	4D.914
Sutherland Green	4D.904	Steel Grey	4D.1302
Royal Blue	4D.388	Alaskan Blue	4D.1303
		Cherry Red	4D.1156

AUSTIN COMMERCIAL RANGE

Spruce Green	4D.813
Island Blue	4D.727
Light Red	4D.1134

FORD RANGE

Ivory (1957)	4D.855
Dover White	4D.730
Cirrus White	4D.952
Dorchester Grey (1957)	4D.856
Corfe Grey	4D.593
Newark Grey	4D.747
Brecon Grey	4D.869
Arundel Lilac (Arundel Grey)	4D.734
Vulcan Grey	4D.1266
Smoke Grey	4D.962
Canterbury Green	4D.1235
Hereford Green	4D.670
Ludlow Green	4D.735
Lichen Green	4D.957
Winchester Blue	4D.401
Westminster Blue	4D.493
Sarum Blue	4D.603
Richmond Blue	4D.737
Kenilworth Blue	4D.736
Ambassador Blue (Norwich Blue)	4D.600
Pompadour Blue	4D.963
Shark Blue	4D.961
Bristol Fawn	4D.1236
Wells Fawn	4D.599
Durham Beige	4D.739
Morocco Beige	4D.946
Rochester Red	4D.868
Monza Red (Rougemont Red)	4D.1201
Imperial Maroon	4D.1265
Pembroke Coral	4D.819
Sunburst Yellow (Conway Yellow)	4D.908
Ermine White	4D.984
Linden Green	4D.990
Ming Yellow	4D.1507
Regency Grey	4D.999
Chateau Grey	4D.974
Lime Green	4D.973
Caribbean Turquoise	4D.985
Sapphire Blue	4D.1505

FORD COMMERCIAL RANGE

Ivory	4D.855
Express Blue	4D.1116

Galleon Green	4D.1117
Cargo Grey	4D.741
Rialto Red	4D.866
Merchant Fawn	4D.742
Highway Yellow	4D.870

ROOTES GROUP
HILLMAN/HUMBER GROUP

Cloud White	4D.767
Foam White (Foam Grey)	4D.1137
Moonstone	4D.1212
Golden Sand	4D.405
Thistle Grey	4D.621
Pearl Grey	4D.622
Dawn Mist	4D.632
Fathom Grey	4D.708
Astral Grey	4D.709
Charcoal	4D.1138
Summer Blue	4D.623
Fiesta Blue	4D.765
Windsor Blue	4D.823
Glacier Blue	4D.821
Ocean Blue	4D.1136
Powder Blue	4D.912
Corinth Blue	4D.620
Seacrest Green	4D.659
Sage Green	4D.1271
Antelope	4D.1139
Cavalry Beige	4D.1110
Pippin Red	4D.460
Apple Green	4D.1374
Regency Beige	4D.1377
Caramel	4D.1376
Smoke Green	4D.1172
Glen Green	4D.1375
Lake Blue	4D.1467

COMMER COMMERCIAL COLOURS

Foam White	4D.1137
Thistle Grey	4D.621
Pearl Grey	4D.622
Seacrest Green	4D.659
Apple Green	4D.1374
Glen Green	4D.1375
Fiesta Blue	4D.765
Powder Blue	4D.912
Lake Blue	4D.1467
Antelope	4D.1139
Caramel	4D.1376
Pippin Red	4D.460

SINGER RANGE

Cloud White	4D.767
Pearl Grey	4D.622
Dawn Mist	4D.632
Thistle Grey	4D.621
Fathom Grey	4D.708
Charcoal	4D.1138
Seacrest Green	4D.659
Sage Green	4D.1271
Corinth Blue	4D.620
Summer Blue	4D.623
Windsor Blue	4D.823
Glacier Blue	4D.821
Fiesta Blue	4D.765
Cavalry Beige	4D.1110
Pippin Red	4D.460
Smoke Green	4D.1172
Lake Blue	4D.1467

SUNBEAM RANGE

Moonstone	4D.1212
Thistle Grey	4D.621
Dawn Mist	4D.632
Pearl Grey	4D.622
Ash Grey	4D.1272
Velvet Green	4D.1273
Sage Green	4D.1271
Corinth Blue	4D.620
Summer Blue	4D.623
Fiesta Blue	4D.765
Windsor Blue	4D.823
Glacier Blue	4D.821
Powder Blue	4D.912
Morocco Brown	4D.1274
Pippin Red	4D.460
Lake Blue	4D.1467

MORRIS RANGE

Cream	4D.718
Pale Ivory	4D.911
Clarendon Grey	4D.409
Birch Grey	4D.411
Twilight Grey	4D.506
Dark Grey (Frilford Grey)	4D.928
Smoke Grey (Blue Grey)	4D.1243
Pearl Grey (Off White)	4D.1275
Mist Green	4D.407
Empire Green	4D.410
Light Green (Sage Green)	4D.817
Dark Green	4D.818
Island Green	4D.873

Steel Blue	4D.1135
Turquoise	4D.719
Clipper Blue (Blue)	4D.1245
Red	4D.1134
Maroon	4D.1246
Cherry Red	4D.1156
Old English White	4D.1173
Connaught Green	4D.1322

MORRIS COMMERCIAL RANGE

Birch Grey	4D.411
Frilford Grey	4D.928
Blue Grey	4D.1243
Connaught Green	4D.1322
Beige	4D.1242
Light Red	4D.1134

WOLSELEY RANGE

Birch Grey	4D.411
Smoke Grey	4D.1243
Island Green	4D.873
Porcelain Green	4D.1276
Navy Blue	4D.1277
Clipper Blue (Blue)	4D.1245
Champagne Beige	4D.871
Whitehall Beige	4D.1242
Maroon	4D.1246
Old English White	4D.1173
Connaught Green	4D.1322

M.G. RANGE

Pale Ivory	4D.911
Birch Grey	4D.411
Woodland Green	4D.412
Island Green	4D.873
Steel Blue	4D.1135
Whitehall Beige	4D.1242
Autumn Red	4D.413
Red	4D.1134
Cherry Red	4D.1156

RILEY RANGE

Birch Grey	4D.411
Frilford Grey	4D.928
Woodland Green	4D.412
Autumn Red	4D.413
Maroon	4D.1246
Connaught Green	4D.1322
Old English White	4D.1173

Spray Gun with container

Graining Comb

ROVER RANGE

Ivory	4D.416
Dark Grey	4D.418
Dove Grey (1959)	4D.1218
Light Grey (1959)	4D.1217
Connaught Green	4D.414
Landrover Bronze Green	4D.428
Rush Green	4D.1129
Shadow Green	4D.1128

STANDARD RANGE

Nimbus White	4D.1126
Grey	4D.421
Lichfield Green	4D.899
Cotswold Blue	4D.1105
Powder Blue	4D.1125
Coffee	4D.927

TRIUMPH RANGE

Sebring White	4D.1278
British Racing Green	4D.815
Lichfield Green	4D.899
Powder Blue	4D.1125
Monaco Blue	4D.1279
Targo Purple	4D.1280
Alpine Mauve	4D.1281
Signal Red	4D.1239
Coffee	4D.927

VAUXHALL RANGE

Dover White	4D.895
Imperial Ivory	4D.1131

Farina Grey	4D.896
Horizon Blue	4D.803
Kingfisher Blue	4D.656
Empress Blue	4D.807
Haven Blue	4D.1140
Royal Blue	4D.1141
Wedgwood Blue	4D.898
Morocco Red	4D.657
Gipsy Red	4D.801
Chariot Red	4D.1125
Mountain Rose	4D.897
Shoreline Beige	4D.711
Harvest Yellow	4D.802
Regency Cream	4D.1382
Banff Blue	4D.1381
Maroon	4D.1383
Coronado Yellow	4D.1379
Kewanee Green	4D.1380

BEDFORD COMMERCIAL RANGE

Mist Grey	4D.1463
Fjiord Blue	4D.1422
Honey Beige	4D.1464
Cherry Red	4D.1225

BERGER FLEET COLOURS

Super Black	4D.14
Pale Cream	4D.1478
Mid Coach Green	4D.1479
Mail Red	4D.425
Royal Blue	4D.61
White	4D.63
Berkeley Maroon	4D.1480

CHAPTER 10

PAINTING A MOTOR CYCLE COMBINATION

Repainting a motor cycle combination can be done by spray or brush.

The paintwork may be chipped in places and the gloss faded but, if the actual paintwork is sound, it may not be necessary to strip it. On the other hand if the paint is peeling and badly cracked, it should be stripped. In some cases it may be chipped off with a scraper.

The first job is to take the side-car from the chassis.

Mount the side-car upside-down on a bench or table at a convenient working height. The first thing to do is to deal with the preparation and rubbing, provided no stripping is required.

Take some soapy water and medium abrasive paper, wet the complete surface with a sponge, then rub down as mentioned in Chapter 2 till smooth. It is essential to rub out the edges of breaks or fractions to feather edge them; this helps to give good adhesion to the priming coat.

It is advisable to rub only a small portion of the body at a time. Half of the panels and each ends makes good divisions. Finally wash off with clean water and dry with washleather.

Having wiped the body clean turn it over as soon as possible. If water gets into the inside, sponge this out then turn the body upside-down again. Many modern side-cars have a trimming fixed over the outside of the body, usually finished in a light colour. It is essential to protect this as well as the interior from paint, which may be difficult to remove.

Brown paper fixed with adhesive tape will give protection. The paper should be tucked underneath the body when it is turned upside-down.

THE KEMITONE PROCESS
This should be useful to the amateur painter.

1. *Description*

Kemitone Rust Remover is a solution of mixed acids with good etching properties. Because it is acidic, rubber gloves should be worn during application and when handling it. It is supplied in liquid form, ready for use.

2. *What Rust Remover Will Do*

It will remove all surface rust and thoroughly clean the metal to ensure perfect adhesion of subsequent coats of paint. It will chemically treat the surface of the metal to prevent further rust spread. Rust Remover V.2595 is supplied in stone jars. The sizes available are 1-gallon, ½-gallon, ¼-gallon and 1-pint jars.

3. *Application*

Application is by sponge or brush to the rusted parts. Leave 15-20 minutes for full action of the liquid. If the rust is deeply embedded, two applications may be necessary. While rust remover is on the surface, rub with abrasive or emery paper to help loosen scale.

Wash off thoroughly with water and dry the surface with rags or compressed air. It is important that the sludge is completely removed from all beadings and joints by water washing. Best results are obtained if the work is primed as soon as possible.

COMPLETE PROCESS FROM BARE METAL – STEEL

1. Wipe over the surface with petrol or white spirits to remove dirt or grease, then rub with abrasive and give a good wash down with clean water.
2. Apply a thin coat of Kemitone Oil Primer and allow to dry overnight (12-16 hours).
3. Next fill dents and imperfections with Kemitone Hard Stopper. Allow four hours to dry.
4. Apply one to three coats, as required, of Kemitone Oil Filler, allowing four hours between each coat. Leave the last coat overnight before wet flatting with 280 abrasive paper (finish with 320 paper). Remove all rubbing slush, wash off thoroughly and allow to dry.
5. Apply one coat of Kemitone Undercoat, avoiding heavy application, allow 4-6 hours to dry, then apply a further coat and lightly rub down.
6. Apply one coat of Kemitone Enamel, avoiding heavy application, and allow 6 to 8 hours to dry.

7. Ensure that the enamel is hard dry by leaving overnight. Lightly dry, rub down and apply Kemitone varnish. Rub the enamel only very lightly with fine abrasive. This is sometimes called 'Mossing Down'.

Shortened Process
Where a good commercial finish is required the following shortened process may be used.
1. Clean thoroughly according to the nature of the surface.
2. Apply a thin coat of Kemitone Oil Primer. Allow to dry 12-16 hours (overnight). 'Scuff' or rub lightly to make smooth.
3. Apply one coat of Kemitone Undercoat. Allow to dry four hours. 'Scuff' or rub lightly to remove nibs (bits of roughness).
4. Apply one coat of Kemitone Synthetic Coach Enamel. Allow 6-8 hours for drying.

Complete Process for Wood
1. Clean down thoroughly. Remove all dirt and grease and seal knots with Shellac or Patent Knotting. Allow to dry well.
2. Apply a thin coat of Kemitone Oil Primer. Allow to dry overnight (12-16 hours).
3. Fill dents and imperfections with Kemitone Hard Stopper. Allow four hours to dry.
4. Apply one to three coats as required of Kemitone Oil Filler, allowing four hours between each coat. Leave the last coat overnight before wet flatting with 280 abrasive paper. Remove all rubbing slush, wash off thoroughly, blow out crevices with air if possible, and allow to dry.
5. Apply one coat of Kemitone Undercoat, allow 4-6 hours to dry. Lightly rub down with 320 paper.
6. Apply one coat of Kemitone Enamel, and avoid heavy application. Allow 6-8 hours to dry.
7. Leave the enamel overnight to dry, then lightly rub down or moss down (light rub), wipe clean and apply the varnish coat.

Kemitone can be supplied from stock in 30 different colours, including black and white. Kemitone is particularly resistant to sea air, and the atmosphere of industrial towns. It has good adhesion and combines toughness with great flexibility.

"Materials made by Lewis Berger, London."

CHAPTER 11

MISCELLANEOUS
THINGS YOU SHOULD KNOW

The Reason for Painting

The bodywork of a car is subject to much wear and tear. It has to stand up to the hot sun, cold weather, fog, frost and snow. Thousands of cars have no garages.

The paintwork undergoes a great strain. Tar clings to the surface and if not carefully washed off damages it.

Moisture is the enemy of paintwork. When paint is chipped away, as so often happens by accident, bare metal is exposed and moisture penetrates. In a matter of hours the action between metal and moisture sets up rust. If this is not checked it begins to creep under the paint film. It is only a matter of months and the paint begins to peel away. A touch of paint in time prevents this.

A car must be painted to keep rust away and to give the bodywork a long life. Not only does paint give protection, it promotes smartness as well. Paint is always a good investment.

What is Paint?

Paint is a mixture of pigment (coloured, yet solid). It is mixed with a vehicle (thinners or medium which may be raw or boiled linseed oil, turpentine, liquid driers) and varnish.

Today paint manufacturers have their own formulas for making paint; the nature of the oils, pigments and varnishes are secret.

When paint is applied to a suitably prepared surface, either by spray or brush, chemical actions are set up between the air and the constituents. This passes through various stages until the paint dries out in a solid film. Paint applied to metal dries out through evaporation. Paint itself is distinct from enamel. Paint has only a moderate gloss; it is opaque and shows brushmarks. Enamel has better flowing qualities, being made with a good per cent of varnish. But there is little difference today between gloss paint and enamel.

Varnish

Varnish is a transparent or pigmented coating. It consists of a number of resins or oils. There are dozens of different brands of varnish on the market today. They include clear cellulose, oil, synthetic, and spirit varnish. Varnish protects wood or metal and renews the life of all paintwork.

Why Abrasives Must Be Used

In all good class paintwork, the resurfacer and undercoats must be made smooth. This gives a key, which is most important, for it helps the finishing paint to grip the surface.

Steel wool, dry and waterproof abrasives, glasspaper and emery paper are the main abrasives. Waterproof abrasive papers consist of carborundum silicate secured to a backing paper with a waterproof adhesive. The paper can be used wet or dry.

The abrasive paper backings are graded in weight. 60, 80 and 100 are for rough rubbing and cleaning. 150, 180, 220 and 280 are for the finer rubbing. These waterproof abrasives are essential today when using modern synthetic enamels and celluloses, where high class finishing is required.

Remarks on Cellulose

Although cellulose enamels are ideal for car refinishing they are not suitable for wooden surfaces. The pigment is very finely ground. These enamels are mostly applied by spray and the coating is thin. This often leads to a lack of 'build'. Cellulose enamel does not obscure the grain of wood satisfactorily. Consequently the 'build up' prior to the cellulose finish has to be done with fillers before refinishing with cellulose enamel.

Wood shrinks and contracts, and these movements make the cellulose coating flake. With a metal surface it is different; there is little movement, the cellulose mainly drying by evaporation.

Cellulose enamels have a very low flashpoint. *Always be on guard against fire.* A warm atmosphere is essential when spraying cellulose; coldness causes a loss of gloss. Cellulose should be kept in an outside store. A steel locker is ideal for this.

THE IMPORTANCE OF PAINT BRUSHES

Although more and more people today are using spray guns, the paint brush is most important, even though there is a tendency for some people to give it second place. The paint brush will always play an important part in first-class painting. A great number of commercial vehicles are still brush-painted. This finish can equal if not surpass that of the spray gun.

For high-class work the quality of brushes must be good. In selecting a good brush, the length of the bristles and thickness must be considered.

To test the bristles of a brush pull one out and set light to it. If the bristle burns away and leaves ash, it is a pure bristle. If the bristle flares up and disappears, it is inferior or vegetable fibre suitable only for rough work.

The best quality brushes in use today are varnish brushes. They are oval in shape, bound in tin, and rubber set. The bristles are ground away to a chisel edge. This type of brush is ready for use immediately.

All loose hairs should be worked out of a brush immediately before putting it into use. Comb through the bristles with a fine comb, or use it as a duster for a time. Overnight soaking in clean water will also remove loose bristles. Many sprayers prefer to put on the priming coat with a brush. The reason for this is that the paint can be well rubbed into the surface.

Solvents

Another name for solvents is thinners. This can be confusing to the amateur painter bearing in mind there are several types of thinners; these being used for cellulose, oil paint, synthetic, French polish and spirit paints.

The main thinners in use today are cellulose thinners for cellulose, white spirits and turpentine for synthetics and oil paints, methylated spirits for shellac, French polish and spirit quick-drying paints.

The words thinner and solvent mean practically the same. Each thinner will dissolve or mix with its own particular paint or pigment. Solvent or thinners may also include petrol and paraffin, useful for removing grease and cleaning.

It is sometimes dangerous to use inflammable solvents or thinners for cleaning. On many jobs sugar soap will give satisfactory results.

For the washing down of greasy metal the solutions should be as strong as possible. After cleaning the metal should be neutralized. It should be washed over with clean warm water and dried off in a warm atmosphere before paint is applied. Caustic soda is also suitable for removing heavy coatings of grease if the object to be painted is immersed in it overnight. Caustic soda is not suitable for cleaning aluminium.

Brushmarks

It is very difficult to avoid brushmarks when laying off undercoats, which are flat paints, their object being to obscure blemishes and build up a good surface.

Undercoats seldom run, but they dry off quickly. There is a tendency to brush the paint on the surface too thickly. This shows brush marks when drying out. Brush marks are not difficult to remove; a quick rub down with wet abrasive paper and soapy water will level them out. The surface must be wiped dry afterwards.

Undercoats or resurfacer coats should be applied in equal thickness to the whole surface. The coating should be on the thin side, then brushmarks will be avoided.

The old coachpainters relied a great deal on flatting down to remove brushmarks. Provided the rubbing down is done well the finishing coat, being glossy, will eliminate minor marks.

Why the Job Should Be Kept Clean

Dirt and dust have always been the painter's enemy. For instance, work may have been prepared well, stripped, cleaned, primed, stopped and undercoated. Throughout these stages the paint must dry without dirt or dust settling on it. Dirt or dust makes the paintwork bitty and rough. Paint should also be free from bits and should be strained if necessary.

It is important to keep brushes clean, free from bits or lint from rags or clothing. Priming and undercoating can be rubbed down to a certain extent; this eliminates roughness caused through dust and dirt. With the finishing paint, however, it is much more difficult. After flatting it will need recoating; this causes extra work and the finish will not be so good.

Try to avoid things that cause dust and dirt; for instance, air currents carry minute particles of dust which get attached to wet paint. They cannot be dealt with until the paint is dry. Put your brushes down in a clean place; it is surprising the amount of dirt brushes pick up. All finishing should be done in a thoroughly clean place.

When a Quick Finish is Needed

Many second-hand cars are purchased today looking quite shabby, yet the paintwork despite its lack of gloss is in a fair condition. The foundation for all standard cellulose work is an oil-based primer followed by stopping, filling, resurfacing, wet rubbing down, and finishing with cellulose enamel.

Provided the primer is sound, the work can go on from here when a quick repaint is needed. One or two coats of cellulose resurfacer can be sprayed at half-hourly intervals. Allow two hours' hardening time, then rub down with medium abrasive paper.

When all is nicely dried off spray on cellulose enamel. Leave the work overnight, then flat down with wet abrasive paper, using soapy water as a lubricant to level spray marks. A final coat of cellulose spraying after the wet rubbing will leave the surface ready for polishing.

Never polish cellulose until the new paintwork has stood twenty-four hours after spraying. Polishing means loss of gloss if carried out too soon. Clean rags of the muslin type are best for polishing, but there is no short cut to success in this. Plenty of elbow grease is needed to get that plate-glass finish, but it is surprising what patience and a little time will do.

Correct Spraying Distance

Many amateur sprayers forget to stand the correct distance from their work when operating the spray gun. This is often because the distance from the gun to the work must vary with material being sprayed.

When spraying thick paints the gun should be held closer to the work than when using thinner materials. Thin mixtures leave the gun speedily; if the gun is held too close the paint will run. If the gun is held too far away a full wet coat will not be applied and the paint will lose its gloss. The average distance the gun should be held from the work is 9 to 10 inches. Experience will help the sprayer to get the correct distance.

The gun should be held parallel to the work when spraying, but the method of spraying may differ according to the type of job in hand.

Spraying or Brushing

The choice of the spray or brush depends upon circumstances, whether the job lends itself better to spraying or brushing, or whether the materials are more suitable for spray work; or if there is good ventilation.

Can the synthetic enamel be better put on by brush than spray, or by a combination of both? Or can the priming be better applied by brush because it can be rubbed into the surface?

Some materials are difficult to apply by brush, owing to the possibility of brush marks; such materials are more successfully applied by spray. Other materials which are difficult to spray in a flowing manner without runs can be brushed on more easily.

The combined use of spray and brush depends much upon the painter. There is no reason why the brush should not be a useful ally to the spray gun. Provided good materials are used good work can be done with both.

After Painting

Four to eight weeks after painting all that is required is normal washing of the paintwork with plenty of clean water. A soft sponge should be used for this; it will not scratch the paint.

After this period the finish should be hard enough to take the full strength of polish. Washing and polishing in time will remove dirt or tar. This may have caused some annoyance when the job was first painted.

It sometimes happens that one or two places are revealed which need touching up. Flat these parts down with fine abrasive and soap and water. Avoid scratching and vigorously polishing till the real gloss returns. Trouble and labour will be found to be worthwhile when the real beauty of the finish is revealed.

NEW ACRYLIC PAINTS

Any keen do-it-yourselfer would be the first to recognize that it is important to follow a manufacturers instructions and we feel we should add a word of warning for those fortunate to own a 1965 model.

Recent technical research into resins and pigments has resulted in the development of a new range of paint materials based on the use of an acrylic man-made resin.

Most of use are familiar with the p.v.c. made household utensils, telephones and even false teeth which are all derived from resins of the acrylic family and it is this basic resin which as been adapted for use as a coating for motor cars.

In the U.S.A. acrylic enamels have been used for some years and the 1964 Vauxhall range were the first British cars to be coated in these new materials.

Now most British manufacturers have 1965 models which are coated in acrylics.

The motorist has quite a lot to gain because acrylics are extremely tough and durable and do not need polishing and, in fact, the car will keep its polish by simply washing down with water and a little detergent.

Another major plus point is that the car will not lose its colour as the water white acrylic resin is unaffected by the ultra-violet content of normal daylight which does so much damage to nitro-cellulose based car paints.

In the past it has been very difficult to remove minor scratches and abrasions but now it is possible to polish these out with a power operated mop.

Nevertheless, this will pose a problem for the keen motorist who wishes to carry out paint repairs.

The car manufacturers state that these new models should only be repaired with an air-drying acrylic enamel.

This does suggest that if you own a 1965 motor car and you are involved in major paint repairs you would be well advised to contact your local garage or agent before tackling the job.

However, minor damage can often be corrected by polishing out the defect but if the damage is more extensive acrylic enamels in aerosol cans can be purchased from most accessory shops.

These new acrylic paints are applied in exactly the same way as the nitro-cellulose types.

If a re-spray is contemplated, then the materials can be purchased from most motor factors or if you are in any difficulty, your local garage can provide you with the name of his supplier.

Never repair these new cars with a nitro-cellulose based repair enamel. Although you may get a satisfactory job at first, the nitro-cellulose will eventually discolour in sunlight and your repair patch will become very obvious.

If you are in any doubt at all consult your nearest garage.